# The Museum of PHOBIAS

## The ALARMING ANIMAL Collection

By JOHN WOOD
AND
DANIELLE JONES

Gareth Stevens
PUBLISHING

Please visit our website, www.garethstevens.com.
For a free color catalog of all our high-quality books,
call toll free 1-800-542-2595 or fax 1-877-542-2596.

**Cataloging-in-Publication Data**

Names: Wood, John. | Jones, Danielle.
Title: The alarming animal collection / John Wood and Danielle
Jones.
Description: New York : Gareth Stevens Publishing, 2021. | Series:
The museum of phobias | Includes index.
Identifiers: ISBN 9781538259948 (pbk.) | ISBN 9781538259962
(library bound) | ISBN 9781538259955 (6 pack)
Subjects: LCSH: Phobias–Juvenile literature. | Animals–Juvenile
literature.
Classification: LCC RC535.W66 2021 | DDC 616.85'225–dc23

First Edition

Published in 2021 by
**Gareth Stevens Publishing**
111 East 14th Street, Suite 349
New York, NY 10003

© 2021 Booklife Publishing
This edition is published by arrangement with Booklife Publishing

Written by: John Wood
Edited by: Madeline Tyler
Designed by: Danielle Jones

Printed in the United States of America

CPSIA compliance information: Batch #CS20GS: For further information contact Gareth
Stevens, New York, New York at 1-800-542-2595.

# The Museum of PHOBIAS

## CONTENTS

# MUSEUM

Oh, hello – we haven't had a visitor to this museum in a long time. This is very surprising. I hope you are feeling brave.

I'm sure you know what it's like to be scared. Your heart races, your legs shake, and your stomach feels sick. However, lots of people get very scared of things that are not frightening to most other people. These fears are called phobias. Phobias can be tricky to deal with.

Having a phobia is more than being a bit scared. Phobias are serious fears of something, even if there is no real danger. Phobias can have a big effect on people's lives.

Scientists aren't completely sure why we get phobias. Where do these fears come from? Why do our brains find some harmless things so scary? People have phobias of all sorts of things, as you will soon find out.

All the things you see in this museum were sent in from people all around the world. These phobias are real. Are you ready to walk through these rooms and understand a little bit more about what scares people the most?

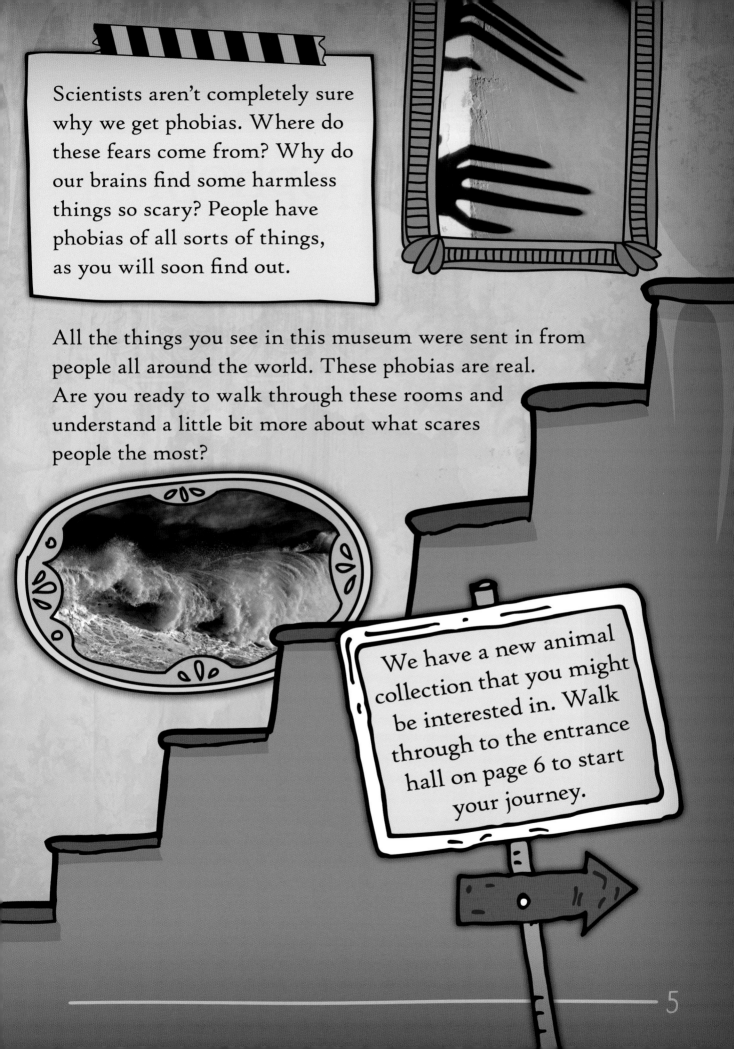

We have a new animal collection that you might be interested in. Walk through to the entrance hall on page 6 to start your journey.

# Ophidiophobia

*noun*

(oh – fih – dee – oh – foh – bee – ah)

## Is a snake scary because of how it moves?

It slithers and slides. Its scaly body winds and twists around a tree or a rock – or an arm. Is a snake scary because of its fangs? Or is it the forked tongue that flicks quickly, tasting the air, looking for food? Some people are scared of the cold, black eyes. Others are scared of how it might feel to touch it. Or maybe it is the way this legless animal lurches forward to strike, faster than you can move. Your legs shake just thinking about it. This is ophidiophobia, the fear of snakes.

Some snakes are venomous. This means they can inject an animal with a deadly substance called venom when they bite. Venom is very dangerous.

The green anaconda is the biggest snake in the world.

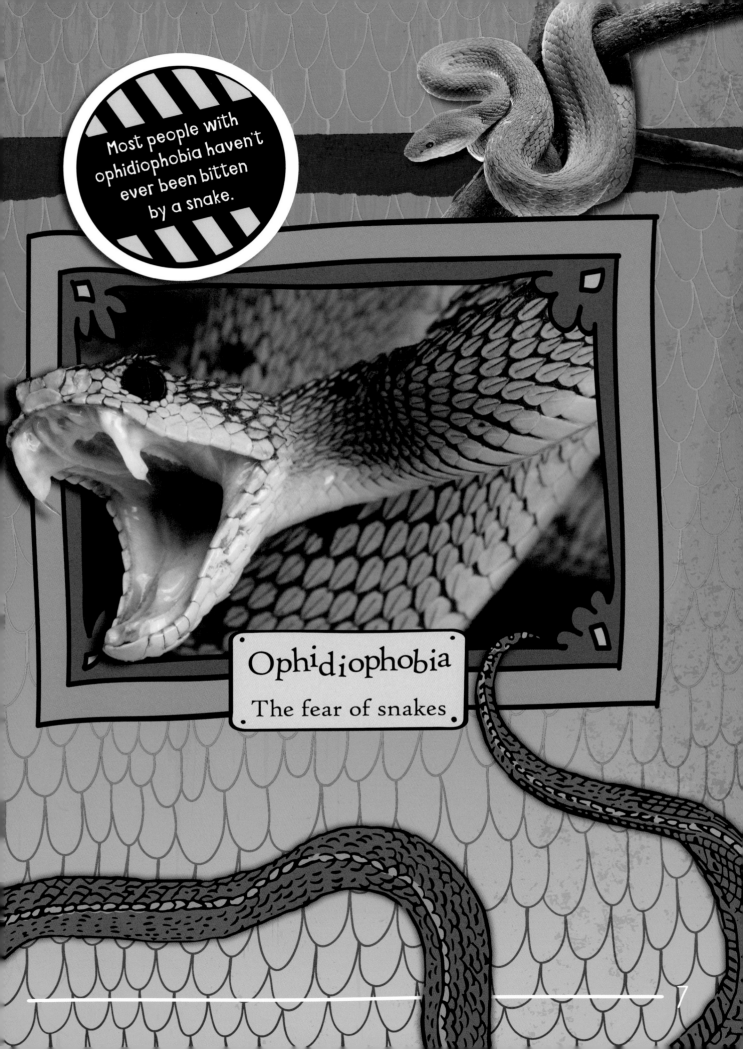

Most people with ophidiophobia haven't ever been bitten by a snake.

Ophidiophobia

The fear of snakes

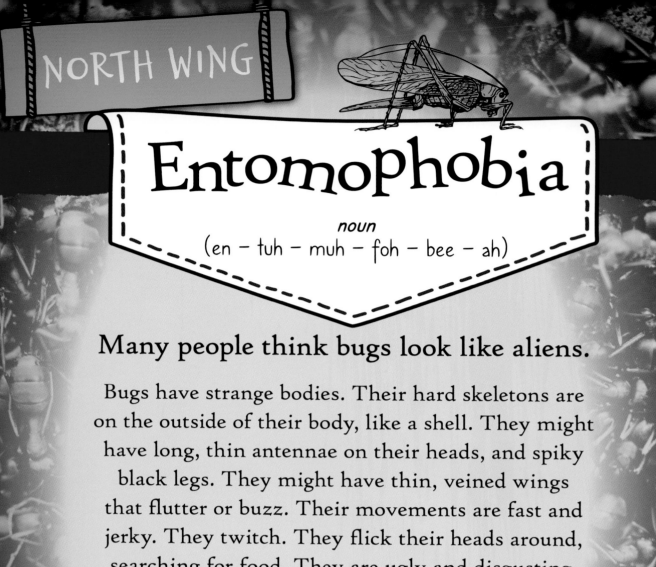

# Entomophobia
### noun
(en – tuh – muh – foh – bee – ah)

**Many people think bugs look like aliens.**

Bugs have strange bodies. Their hard skeletons are on the outside of their body, like a shell. They might have long, thin antennae on their heads, and spiky black legs. They might have thin, veined wings that flutter or buzz. Their movements are fast and jerky. They twitch. They flick their heads around, searching for food. They are ugly and disgusting. They crawl over food and tables, or under toilet seats. They creep around, just out of sight. They are in your house. You feel them on your body. Your heart beats faster and faster. This is entomophobia, the fear of insects.

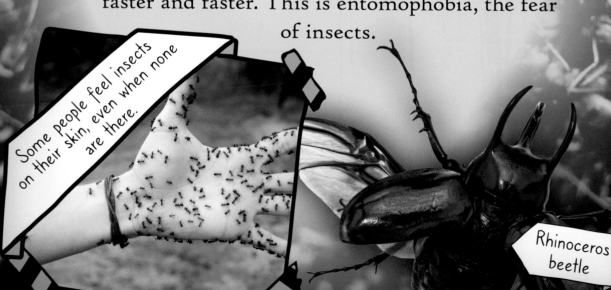

Some people feel insects on their skin, even when none are there.

Rhinoceros beetle

**Entomophobia**
The fear of insects

Entomophobia is a fear of all sorts of bugs, such as bees, flies, cockroaches, beetles, and ants.

# Hippophobia

*noun*

(hip – oh – foh – bee – ah)

### Have you ever seen a horse at night?

It stands tall. It is quiet. But it is powerful – horses have strong hooves and a dangerous kick. Maybe it is this power and strength that scares some people. These animals can run quickly and pull heavy things. They bite and bolt. Just looking at them can make people feel sick with worry. They are afraid they will meet a bad-tempered horse. Who knows – just because a horse has a saddle doesn't mean it isn't wild at heart. It could lash out at any moment. This is hippophobia, the fear of horses.

Arabian stallion

People with hippophobia might also be scared of other animals with hooves.

The biggest horse ever recorded was over 7 feet (2.13 m) tall from shoulder to hoof. A man is usually around 5 foot 9 inches (1.75 m) from head to foot.

# Hippophobia
The fear of horses

11

# SCIENCE CENTER

## Fight, Flight, Freeze

Your body has a built-in defense for scary situations. It is called the fight, flight, freeze response (response is another word for answer). When something scary happens to you, your body does one of these three things:

### FIGHT

Your body gets ready for a fight. You might feel angry or violent and the muscles in your body tense up, ready to lash out at anything dangerous.

### FLIGHT

Your body gets ready to run away. Your heart beats faster and you breathe quicker to give your muscles the energy they need to escape from the danger.

### FREEZE

You feel like you can't move or think. Scientists think this might be your body trying to play dead or block out the scary thing.

The fight, flight, freeze response was very useful to humans who lived in the wild thousands of years ago.

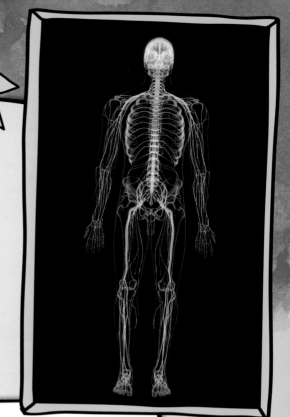

The fight, flight, freeze response is very important for humans. However, sometimes your body and brain get confused about what is a dangerous situation and what isn't. When you have a phobia, you get very scared of something that might not be dangerous at all.

For example, horses aren't usually dangerous, but someone with hippophobia might get the fight, flight, freeze response anyway. Their body gets ready for action – their heart beats faster, they breathe quicker, sweat, and feel sick. However, with the right help, many people can realize that their phobias are nothing to be scared of.

Once someone has overcome a phobia, it no longer triggers their fight, flight, freeze response.

# Selachophobia

*noun*

(sel – ak – uh – foh – bee – ah)

## There are over 350 types of sharks.

Some are small, harmless creatures that live quietly in little corners of the ocean. And some are not. Deep in the watery depths, giant sharks glide through the dark, looking for their next meal. Some of them are always sniffing the water for a trace of blood. They have rows of sharp, deadly teeth. They have cold, black eyes. Just thinking about them makes you breathe faster and feel dizzy. These are ancient killing machines – there were sharks on Earth before there were trees. And they are lurking down in the ocean, somewhere, searching for their next kill. This is selachophobia, the fear of sharks.

Sharks have rows and rows of teeth. When one falls out, another comes forward to take its place.

The biggest shark is the whale shark.

If you are worried about sharks, remember that shark attacks are very, very rare. More people are killed by vending machines each year than by sharks.

## Selachophobia
### The fear of sharks

# Doraphobia

*noun*

(dor – uh – foh – bee – ah)

## Imagine a furry creature.

Maybe it is a bear or a wolf. Or maybe it is a dog or a cat. You might think this phobia is about how deadly some of these animals can be. But some people aren't scared of the teeth or the claws. Instead, they are scared of the fur. Imagine running your fingers through the hair – is it rough or is it soft? Does the fur carry diseases or bugs? Is it tangled? You can feel the hard skin underneath. You feel disgusted and your heart beats quicker. This is doraphobia, the fear of animal fur or skin.

People with this phobia stay away from pets.

A mangy dog

People often feel disgusted by fur used for clothing. This might turn into a form of doraphobia.

## Doraphobia
The fear of animal fur or skin

# Zoophobia

*noun*

(zoh – uh – foh – bee – ah)

If you have a phobia of one or more of the animals in this museum, you have zoophobia.

Many animals have something scary about them. Big teeth, sharp claws, speed, strength – all these things are more than enough to make you panic. You find that you are sweating heavily. Maybe it is how different many animals are from us. They can't talk to us. We can't know what they are feeling most of the time. Who knows what is going on behind their glassy eyes? You feel the fear rise up as you are confronted with a living, breathing creature that is so unlike you – it is unknowable and untrustworthy. This is zoophobia, the fear of animals.

Fruit bats

American crocodile

A person with zoophobia might be afraid of all animals or just certain ones.

KEEP OUT.

Zoophobia
The fear of animals

# GENGHIS KHAN

Genghis Khan was one of the most powerful warriors and leaders of all time. He lived from 1162 to 1227. He created the biggest land empire of all time. An empire is a group of countries or areas of land that are all ruled by one person. The empire stretched over a huge part of Asia.

Genghis Khan was born in Mongolia. He came from a humble family. He became a great warrior and brought together all the tribes of Mongolia. Then his army moved outwards and went to war with other countries, including China.

The world's biggest statue of Genghis Khan

Genghis Khan's army was mostly made up of warriors on horseback.

It is said that Genghis Khan was very strong and clever. His army was known for being ruthless and they killed many thousands of people. However, there was another side to this fearsome figure.

## Cynophobia

Genghis Khan was afraid of dogs. This wasn't a complete surprise – the dogs in Mongolia at the time were vicious and strong. However, Genghis Khan feared them even more than most. The fear of dogs is called cynophobia.

Genghis Khan's soldiers would kill everyone they defeated.

Mongolian bankhar dog

# Musophobia

*noun*

(muss – uh – foh – bee – ah)

## Can you hear a scratching sound?

Something is in the walls, or under the floorboards. It scutters and scurries through the house. You can hear tiny feet running. Then, for a second, you see it – something small and furry. It is too quick, and it has already scrambled through a hole in the wall. You hear distant squeaking and you realize what it must be. It is a rat. Your chest feels tight as you begin to panic. Brown and dirty, the rat could be carrying all sorts of diseases. There are probably lots of them, hiding inside the house. You hear them gnaw on the wood in the attic with their tiny, pointy teeth. Your mind is racing with fear. This is musophobia, the fear of rats and mice.

A rat king is many rats that have their tails tangled together. People have been scared of rat kings throughout history.

Brown rats

The fear of mice and rats might have something to do with the fact that wild ones are dirty and carry diseases.

# Musophobia
The fear of rats and mice

# Ostraconophobia

*noun*

(os – tra – kun – uh – foh – bee – ah)

Tails, pincers, slimy insides, shells, claws, antennae – these are some of the body parts you might find on a shellfish.

Shellfish are a group of lots of different animals, such as shrimp, clams, and crabs. Every one of them is just as scary. They look so alien. The idea of eating them makes you feel sick. Just imagine the horrible taste and texture of their soft bodies inside their hard, outer shell. Are they poisonous? Will they make you ill? Your stomach is turning and feeling sick just thinking about those horrible, disgusting creatures from the depths of the ocean. This is ostraconophobia, the fear of shellfish.

Antennae

Lobsters are shellfish.

Many people are scared of shellfish as food. They worry they will get food poisoning.

## Ostraconophobia
The fear of shellfish

# Alektorophobia

*noun*

(a – lek – tuh – ruh – foh – bee – ah)

## Scientists think that chickens came from dinosaurs.

After most of the dinosaurs were wiped out, the few that were left slowly changed. When a type of animal slowly becomes different over millions of years, it is called evolution. If you look at chickens today, you can see how this might be true. They might not have teeth like dinosaurs, but they have a sharp beak, beady little eyes and long, scaly legs. As you watch them stalk around, your mouth feels dry. You feel scared of these modern-day dinosaurs. You imagine them attacking you, pecking at your hands, legs, and face. This is alektorophobia, the fear of chickens.

Some chickens can survive for a short time after having their head cut off. Some chickens have survived up to 15 minutes, while one chicken survived for a year and a half.

Chickens eat plants, grains, insects, and even small animals such as mice.

Some people are so scared that they can't even eat food that contains chicken.

# Alektorophobia

## The fear of chickens

# Arachnophobia

**noun**

(a – rak – nuh – foh – bee – ah)

## For most people, it is the way a spider moves.

Fast, spindly legs needle the ground as they scuttle across the floor. Out of the corner of your eye you see it, black and bristly. The legs are curled slightly, ready to pounce. The body is big and dark. There is a tense moment where you are too scared to move. Suddenly, the legs twitch, and it has scurried out of sight. Where has it gone? It could be anywhere. It doesn't matter if it is dangerous or harmless. Your skin crawls. This is arachnophobia – the fear of spiders.

Tarantulas, such as this one, are a type of big, hairy spider.

Some spiders have a deadly bite, such as this Sydney funnel-web spider. It is one of the deadliest spiders in the world.

In continents such as Europe and North America, around half of women and one-fifth of men say that they are scared of spiders.

## Arachnophobia
The fear of spiders

# HELP POINT

## Different Types of Fears

There are two different types of fears – rational and irrational.

Rational fears make sense. They are healthy, and the thoughts we have are in line with what we see and hear around us.

Irrational fears do not make sense. They are unhealthy. Irrational thoughts and worries are based on things that are unlikely to happen in everyday life.

Many people would say a fear of injections is irrational because injections help us.

It is important to look at our worries and fears and work out which are rational and which are irrational. Knowing that a thought or worry is irrational can take away its power.

# WHAT DO WE FEAR?

Worrying about being run over by a car is rational. Cars are dangerous and roads are all around us. It is healthy to look both ways and be careful when crossing the road. However, being scared of fruit is irrational. Fruit is not dangerous in the way that cars are. It would be unhealthy to be afraid of lunchtime or stay away from the kitchen because there might be fruit.

Your parent, caregiver, or teacher can help you with your fears and worries.

If you have a phobia or any other worries, try talking to an adult you trust. Together you can work out if it is a rational or irrational fear. They can help you worry less and feel better.

## PHOBIAS CAN MAKE US FEEL:

- Sick
- Shaky
- Sweaty
- Very hot or very cold
- Faint or dizzy
- Out of breath
- As though our heart is beating very fast
- As if we can't think properly or remember the right words

# GIFT SHOP AND EXIT

Congratulations – your visit is over.
I hope you sleep well tonight – it might take
a few days to feel better again.

Why not go to the gift shop before you go? Or would you
rather be out of this museum as soon as possible? I can't say
I would blame you. Run along, now...

## INDEX

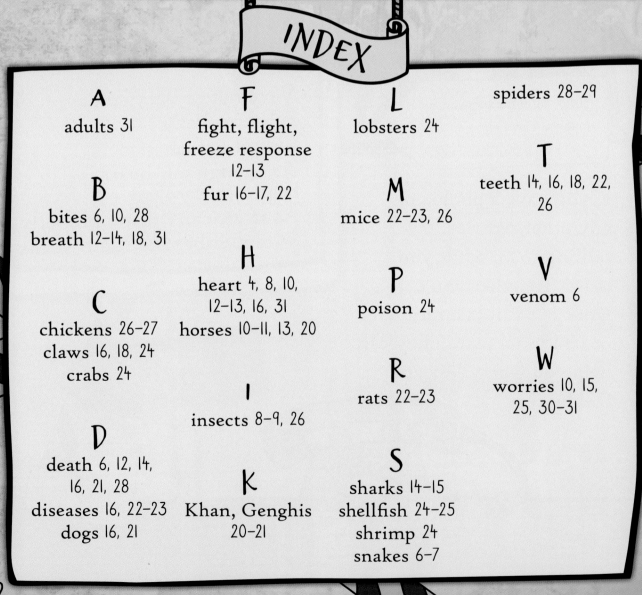